Charlie the Flatulent Christmas Angel

...and Other Stories of Joy

BY STEVE CASE

Illustrations by Brian Scoop Diehl

the apocryphile press
BERKELEY, CA
www.apocryphile.org

apocryphile press
BERKELEY, CA

Apocryphile Press
1700 Shattuck Ave #81
Berkeley, CA 94709
www.apocryphile.org

Printed in the United States of America
ISBN 9781940671468
Text Copyright © 2014 Steve Case
Illustrations Copyright © 2014 Brian Scoop Diehl
All rights reserved.

Contents

Charlie the Flatulent Christmas Angel 5

The Story of the Lost Wise Man 25

Sandra McNeal 28

Clay and Water 32

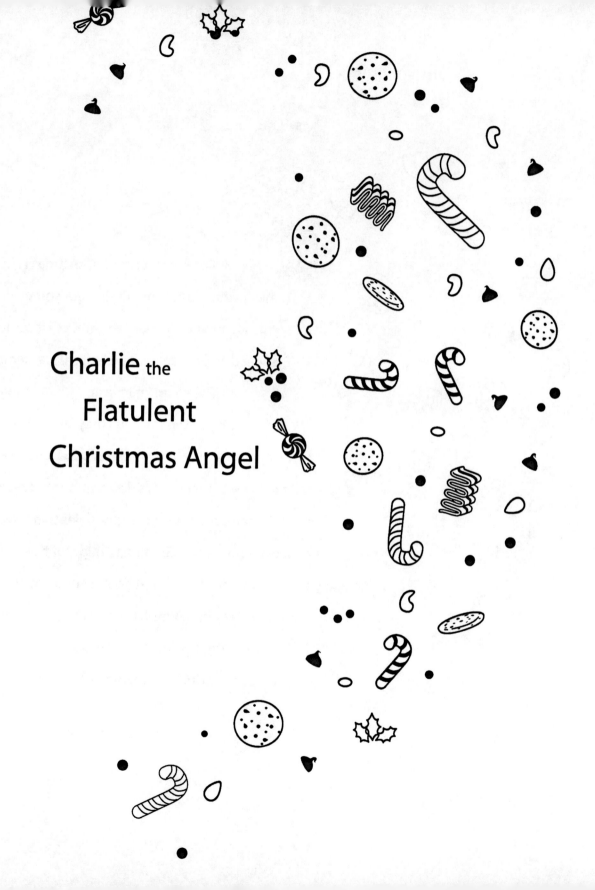

Charlie the
Flatulent
Christmas Angel

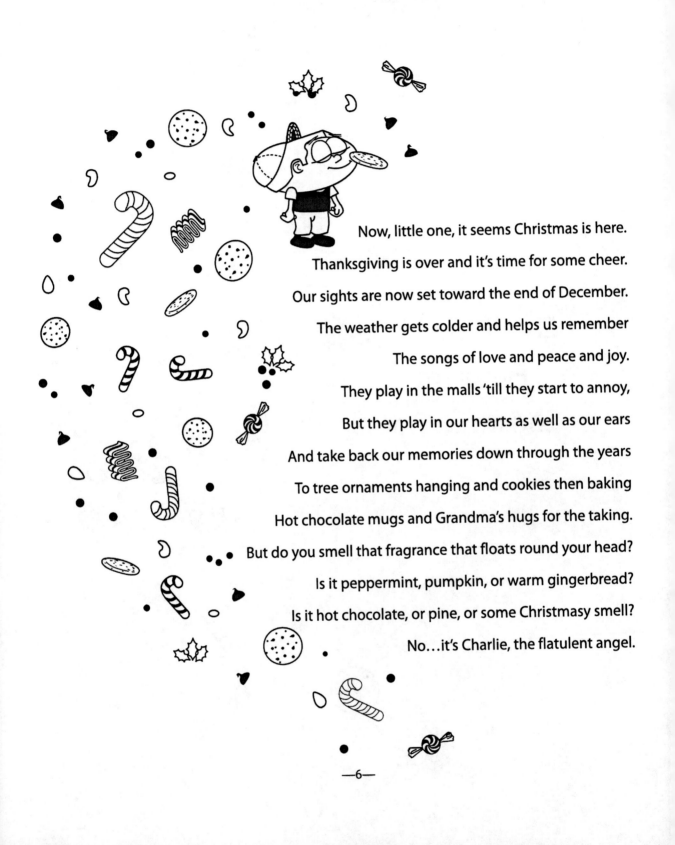

Now, little one, it seems Christmas is here.

Thanksgiving is over and it's time for some cheer.

Our sights are now set toward the end of December.

The weather gets colder and helps us remember

The songs of love and peace and joy.

They play in the malls 'till they start to annoy,

But they play in our hearts as well as our ears

And take back our memories down through the years

To tree ornaments hanging and cookies then baking

Hot chocolate mugs and Grandma's hugs for the taking.

But do you smell that fragrance that floats round your head?

Is it peppermint, pumpkin, or warm gingerbread?

Is it hot chocolate, or pine, or some Christmasy smell?

No…it's Charlie, the flatulent angel.

Now this story, it happened a long time ago,

When Charlie the shepherd boy trudged through the snow

To find his lost lamb who had wandered alone.

Poor little lamb must be chilled to the bone!

But Charlie was good and Charlie was kind.

He went off then searching and he dreamed in his mind

Of the shepherds in stories he heard as a boy,

Of that first Christmas star and the angels of Joy,

And how shepherds brought lambs to the new baby king.

It made Charlie wonder, just what would he bring?

Then he heard the soft bleat of his little lost friend,

Who had slipped and had fallen into the river's west end,

And was washing away with a plaintive "yoo hoo."

But Charlie the shepherd boy knew what to do.

He reached out his hand to the little lost lamb

And remembered again the savior's good plan—

To reach out to the lambs wherever they be.

But poor Charlie slipped and was washed out to sea.

But God was smiling, as God always does,

And God loved the shepherd for all that he was.

God gave him a gift, like no angel before,

A gift that would ban him from the stories of yore,

But a gift nonetheless, a strange Christmas present—

When Charlie broke wind it would always smell pleasant.

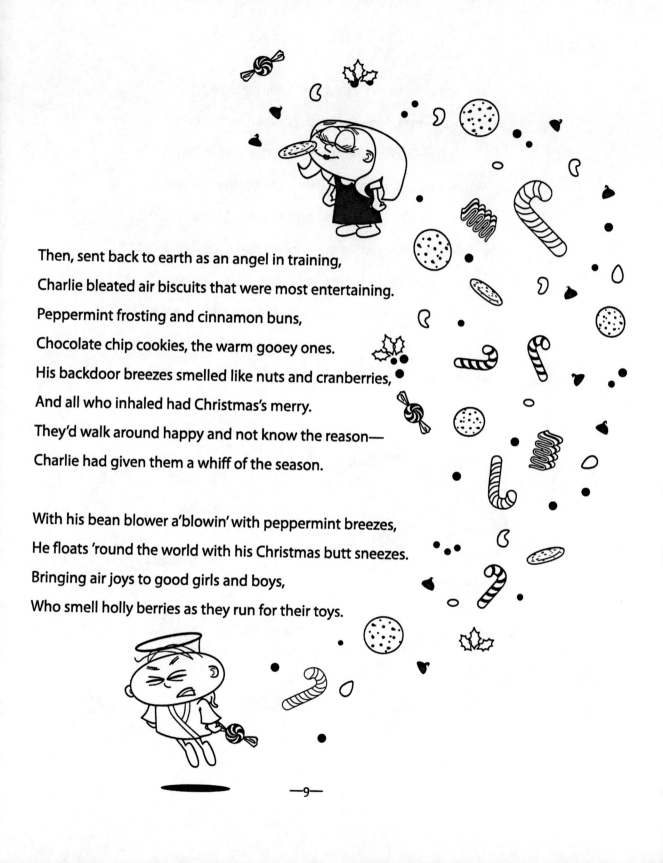

Then, sent back to earth as an angel in training,

Charlie bleated air biscuits that were most entertaining.

Peppermint frosting and cinnamon buns,

Chocolate chip cookies, the warm gooey ones.

His backdoor breezes smelled like nuts and cranberries,

And all who inhaled had Christmas's merry.

They'd walk around happy and not know the reason—

Charlie had given them a whiff of the season.

With his bean blower a'blowin' with peppermint breezes,

He floats 'round the world with his Christmas butt sneezes.

Bringing air joys to good girls and boys,

Who smell holly berries as they run for their toys.

But this story takes place a long time ago,

When the names of your neighbors was a good thing to know,

Before laptop computers and the vast internet,

When a phone on the wall was the best you could get.

In a city called Cleveland on the shores of Lake Erie,

Where despite the cold weather folks were often quite cheery,

At a home filled with orphans with no moms or dads,

No beds for these children, just some worn mattress pads.

No kind daddy stories and no hugs from their mummies.

The cupboards were as empty as the poor children's tummies.

But in that cold place where there was so little to eat

The kids had a spirit that couldn't be beat.

Each night after a supper of rolled oats and bread,

They would place a paper star on top of the head

Of little Bethany Von Beeker, who was then barely five,

And she sat on the shoulders of a big boy called Clive.

The children would stand on some chairs and hold hands

And make their own tree, the best in the land.

They'd make their own ornaments out of bottle caps and string,

And then those poor children would laugh and they'd sing

Of Bethlehem's gifts and the star's wondrous light,

And just before bed they would sing Silent Night.

And as they were singing with their eyes closed up tight

They swore they smelled cookies and sugar delights.

Some smelled pine branches, others smelled pie,

And fragrances floating on the breeze blowing by.

But there was one little thing the kids didn't know

And that was on Christmas they'd be out in the snow.

The lease it was up on their ramshackle house.

Soon they'd be fighting for crumbs with a mouse.

Mr. B. Fizzle Drake

The owner was one Mr. B. Fizzle Drake,

Who'd tear down the house and a high rise he'd make.

Kindness and love are not part of the plan—

Not when your home is owned by a man

Who's so mean and so rotten with snot in his soul.

Why he'd just laugh out loud if you fell in a hole.

—13—

Now just down a few blocks from the orphanage home,

Lived big-hearted Ben whose name was quite known.

A newspaper reporter, back when people read those,

People were quite fond of his newspaper prose.

Ben had a dog, named after Roscoe Lee Brown

And at night they would walk all over town.

But on this night, with Christmas just a few weeks away,

Roscoe broke his leash and he just ran away.

But was he just running? Or was he chasing a scent?

It was one of the cheek-flappers the angel had spent.

Charlie the angel wanted the dog loose,

So he floated a wet one that smelled like cooked goose.

So Roscoe he ran and the reporter ran after

And they ran till they stopped at the sound of kids' laughter,

From inside this ramshackle house falling down.

You didn't hear much laughter from this side of town.

From inside the wall Ben & Roscoe could hear

Sweet voices in song raised in Christmassy cheer.

It wasn't just the music that made them both stop and stare—

Ben caught a whiff of gingerbread air.

Such music, like angels, these children were singing,

Completely unaware of the joy they were bringing.

Now Ben knew this house belonged to B. Fizzle Drake

Who apparently cared nothing for the children at stake.

Why, before the New Year it was cleared for demolition.

"We can't let Drake's plans come to fruition!"

But what could he do? You can't fight city hall—

Not with a dog and some children so small.

You can't change the mind of a heart set in stone

Or stand in front of a bulldozer alone.

You can move the hearts of
newspaper readers

Who might call the mayor or
their council-type leaders.

But B. Fizzle Drake,
he owned half
of the city

You can't pay
the rent with
just a
handful
of pity.

You *could* pay the rent with cash hard and cold.

Ben needed a plan that would be daring and bold.

These kids needed money and they needed it fast.

Now where would a reporter get that kind of cash?

Then on a wind that smelled just like egg nog

Ben found a flier in the mouth of his dog.

It said that on Christmas there was a big talent show.

The kids could all sing on live radio.

They could win the big contest and take the grand prize

And put it in front of Drake's beady eyes.

Ben could save these poor orphans.

He'd put them up on the stage.

But what if they lost out to B. Fizzle's rage?

It was a chance he would take, and he knocked on the door

And sat down with the kids, who sat on the floor.

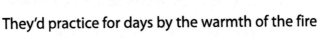

He told them the plan to save their poor home,

To win the prize money and pay off the loan.

They'd practice for days by the warmth of the fire

Their sweet little voices raised up to inspire.

Oh, the story he'd write for his readership huge!

They'd vote for the children and they'd vote out the scrooge.

"But would that be enough?" he thought, doubting his writing.

Could his words be the cause of a city uniting?

Just above Ben, floating over his right shoulder

Was the cheese-cutting angel, who just popped a boulder

And filled the whole room with the scent of cocoa.

These children would never be tossed out in the snow—

Not when the flatulent angel was here,

And Roscoe the dog, and the children's good cheer.

But Ben was just one reporter and they were just kids.

Would that keep them all from hitting the skids?

None of them knew about their angel above,

Whose blaring bum trumpet was a sign of God's love.

And so the orphans all gathered on a cold Christmas eve

Inside of the station to earn their reprieve.

The reporter's kind words would show people still cared.

Then a sign lit up red. "Shhhhh. *On the air.*"

The kids closed their eyes and they opened their hearts

And sang pitch perfect notes in harmony parts.

The songs that they sang went out over the city,

And people looked up from the streets dark and gritty

And heard those sweet voices raised in beautiful song

Like choirs of angels in a heavenly throng.

Was it enough to make them move to their phones

And call in their votes for this group of unknowns?

—19—

Now, just outside of the radio station

Was that toot-scooting angel, whose angelic flotation

Carried him up into that cold Cleveland sky,

Above the whole city and the skyscrapers high.

He clenched his whole body and his cheeks he clapped tight

He blew his bum trumpet and shot off in the night.

With his buttock bassoon he blew scents of pure joy

To all of the grown-ups, and the girls and the boys.

They all smelled the Christmas that made their hearts light

Of candy and cookies and kitchen delights,

Of turkey and biscuits and hot Christmas punch,

Of Cranberry and oranges and caramel corn crunch,

And those cookies with the chocolate kiss in the center,

All from the bum of the angelic presenter.

Across the whole city they smelled hot cinnamon scones.

The people stood up and they ran for their phones

To vote for these children and their anthems so sweet

While smelling hot chocolate and other good things to eat.

They weren't even aware of why they were moved to their phones.

It was more than the paper and the children's sweet tones.

It was the work of the angel, and his Christmassy cloud.

His moon gas, his mud duck, his fluffy out loud.

Why if it wasn't for Charlie and his sweet sphincter song,

The whole Christmas contest might have gone horribly wrong.

Instead, when the numbers were finally tallied,

The children had *won* and their fans they had rallied

To not only give them their prize money won,

But see that their Christmas was second to none.

The children went home, and to their surprise,

They found a crowd waiting with tools and supplies.

The people fixed up their house and cooked for them too.

One lady even adopted a few.

What of B. Fizzle Drake? His plans were now thwarted.

He got his own present, so the paper reported,

Wrapped up in paper and a tag laminated.

And there in the box? Well, I think Roscoe made it.

And Charlie the angel, who tooted with cheer,

Went back into heaven until Christmas next year.

So when you gather round with your loved ones this season,

And you smell those sweet smells but you don't know the reason,

You can be sure that Charlie is near...

Popping a fluffy of sweet Christmas cheer.

The Story of the Lost Wise Man

You know the story of the wise men three,

Who traveled from afar

Across the desert, through the hills,

Following a star.

One king brought gold,

Another myrrh,

And frankincense the third.

They followed a star and a legend old,

Though a map would be preferred.

But there was a fourth who also went

And with the others traveled.

He went back home to feed the cat

And then his trip unraveled.

The other three, all kings of wealth,

Had set out toward the light.

They said, "Hey, let him catch up,"

And soon were out of sight.

The poor lost wise man, now far behind,

He failed to make the connection.

It just goes to show that even then

Men didn't ask directions.

Just the one lone king, all by himself,

Following the light,

He passed the others as they went home

But missed them in the night.

He journeyed on, alone for years

Still yet to give his gift.

The little babe, by now a child,

And his wife, back home, real miffed.

Some say he is out there still

Wandering in the stars.

He hears us gripe about Christmas gifts

And the way we park our cars.

He hears us moan about Christmas cards

And making Christmas lists.

He hears us talk about annoying songs

And all the sales we missed.

He never found the little babe,

Never found the cattle stall.

He's looking for Jesus in the stars.

We're looking in the mall.

So reach out and take hold of a hand

Upon this Holy Night.

And if you find yourself lost

Just start following the light.

Sandra McNeal

It was Sandra McNeal's first day of school

Of her junior class year and she knew well the rules.

Don't be late. Don't use drugs. Put the cell phone away.

Do your homework. Join a club, and just get through the day.

"This year will be different," she had told her reflection,

After a summer of work and deep introspection.

She'd grown tired of the view from the back of the room.

Two years to go and she'd be gone.

Out.

Zooooom.

Armed with a schedule and her student ID

And a book bag that weighed in at one hundred and three.

Her classes were hard, but the teachers mostly cool,

Except for AP English with Mr. O'Toole,

Who was rumored to have, if you looked in his car,

The beating heart of a student, which he kept in a jar.

She would sing in the choir and join Spanish club

And try out for the play despite last year's cold snub.

It was Sandra McNeal's Junior Class year!

A new attitude and nothing to fear.

She put her hand on the door and for just a second or two

She allowed all that fear and stress to come through.

Clutching that handle, she let her mind wail

And saw that big flashing sign. One word. *Fail*.

She allowed all those fears to sink down to her bone

And then she remembered, "I'm never alone.

I've got friends. I've got family. I've got God on my side.

And while that old Sandra may have just sat down and cried.

I am *not* going to listen to those negative voices.

I won't give up that quick. I won't. I have choices.

I choose to live with a garbage-free soul.

I won't be sucked down into high school's black hole.

I won't be caught up in gossipy jabbing

Or hang out with people who make a sport of back-stabbing.

I'm focused. I'm ready. My goals are quite clear.

That's what I'll do with my junior class year.

Junior year. Senior year. Then I'm ready to go.

I'll be off to college and see what they know.

And that dream starts here at the door of my school.

I won't listen to people who say I'm not cool.

Their opinion is crap and, sorry, I just don't have the time.

The only opinion that counts here is mine.

I get to decide who I hang with and don't.

And cut loose the people filled with "Can't do" and "Won't."

You don't have the right to tell me I can't.

I am Sandra McNeal and this is my rant.

This is *my* year and my star will be blazing.

Yes, it'll be hard but also amazing.

You can't stop me now. I'll cut through like a knife."

Then she opened the door...

And walked into her life.

Clay and Water

The old man looked like someone's grandfather

As he quietly worked on the wheel of a potter.

She stared at his hands and the clay and the water.

She had come there to ask his advice.

She said, "Sometimes I feel like the color of beige

Like a bowl of oatmeal or a dark, empty stage.

It's like my whole life is just a blank empty page

So I came here to ask your advice.

I mean, did you feel like this when you were like me,

Right at the beginning of all that could be,

But you couldn't get started and you couldn't quite see

What your life was really about?"

But the potter was silent and stared at the wheel

And her anger boiled up and it was like he could feel

The pain in her heart that she tried to conceal,

But her hands kept clenching into fists.

The wheel kept on turning, the way it will go,

And the lump in his hand started to grow.

He said, "Why are you asking for what you already know?

Don't you know how amazing you are?

There is just one creator and he knows what to do.

Listen to my words, girl, and know that they're true.

He made the grass green and he made the sky blue.

But there's some things you must do for yourself.

This clay is soft, but given the time,

I can work with it slowly with these old hands of mine.

And I can make me a vase or a jug for my wine

But you see, girl, it's all up to me.

You've been given this life and it's already amazing.

You can study your books or spend it stargazing;

You can go out on the road and spend it hell-raising.

But you see, girl, it's all up to you.

But I'll tell you right now, there are people backstage

Who see your empty canvas. They see your blank page,

And they come out here with paint...and mud...and buckets of rage,

And they'll tell who *they* think you are.

They'll push you and mold you like the clay on this wheel

And they won't care a jot about how you might feel.

I promise you, girl, it's your soul that they steal.

But you won't let them have it, will you?

You better define yourself before someone else does.

They follow you around and start flappin' their jaws

But you don't have to listen to them, girl, because

The creator left it all up to you.

Don't go around blaming your mommy or dad,

Your sister who's prettier or your brother the grad

'Cause they had all the same choices you know that you had

It's your life, girl, not anyone else's."

And she looked down inside, deeper than she could remember,

Down where the fire had grown cold as December.

And she saw the small spark, a dim glowing ember,

And she quietly gave it a blow.

And that one tiny coal, it started to glow,

And it made a small flame that started to grow,

And then a bonfire and a growing volcano

And she knew it was just getting started.

It was a note, then a song, then a full symphony,

Backed up by a storm on the crashing blue sea.

She kept it all in her heart, right where it should be,

And she turned to the old man and said,

"I am a dancer or poet or great engineer,

I can build you a building or quote you Shakespeare,

And I have *no* time for those who would fill me with fear.

I know now it's all up to me.

And I'm not a mug or a bowl on your wheel.

I am the wheel itself and I know what I feel.

I'm creating myself and now here's the deal...

I'm ready to define myself."

CPSIA information can be obtained
at www.ICGtesting.com
Printed in the USA
LVOW09s2315211117

557261LV00003B/64/P